Zen

Heal Your Life, Make Friends with Your Emotions and Feel at Peace with Yourself

(Zen for Beginners)

By Maya Faro

Copyright Maya Faro© 2016

All rights reserved. No part of this publication may be reproduced, stored in a retrieval system, or transmitted, in any form or by any means, electronic, mechanical, photocopying, recording or otherwise, without the prior written permission of the author and the publishers.

The scanning, uploading, and distribution of this book via the Internet or via any other means without the permission of the author is illegal and punishable by law. Please purchase only authorized electronic editions, and do not participate in or encourage electronic piracy of copyrighted materials.

Maya Faro © Copyright 2016 - All rights reserved.

Legal Notice:

This book is copyright protected. It for personal use only.

Disclaimer Notice:

Please note the information contained in this document is for educational and entertainment purposes only. Every attempt has been made to provide accurate, up to date and completely reliable information. No warranties of any kind are expressed or implied.

Readers acknowledge that the author is not engaging in the rendering of legal, financial, medical or professional advice. By reading this document, the reader agrees that under no circumstances are we responsible for any losses, direct or indirect, which are incurred as a result of the use of information contained within this document, including, but not limited to, errors, omissions, or inaccuracies.

Table of Contents

Introduction 9
A Brief History of Zen 13
The World of Illusions 21
Lifting the Veil of Illusions................................28
Zen: The Importance of Clear Seeing 33
Who Are You?...36
The Center of the Universe is called "I" 41
Zen in Daily Life 48
Bonus Chapter: The Joy of Mindfulness 54
Conclusion... 60

Introduction

We are what we think.

All that we are arises

with our thoughts.

With our thoughts we

make the world.

(from the

Dhammapada)

There once was a man who was walking along a road when he saw from the distance a horse and its rider approaching toward him. The man could see that the horse was running wildly and so he stepped to the side of the road for safety.

As the horse came closer, the man could see that the rider was someone he knew; it was his friend. His friend was trying to hold on as he rode by. "Where are you going?" said the man to his friend. His friend replied, "I do not know, ask the horse."

This is a Zen story that is a metaphor for how lives are when we live with an undisciplined mind. The horse in the story is a metaphor for our minds, with all their thoughts, beliefs, and conditioning that take control of our lives. Just the like the rider in the story, so many of us live in a reactive manner toward life. Instead of taking control of our lives, we allow our undisciplined minds to determine the direction that we are going.

Even when we are aware that our thoughts are preventing us from moving toward the happiness that we desire, we still often struggle against our minds. The reason for this struggle leads to another Zen metaphor, that of the teacup. You cannot pour tea into a teacup if the teacup is full of tea already, adding more tea will simply cause the tea in the cup to overflow.

Our minds are like the teacup; we cannot transcend the limitations of our mind by just adding more thoughts and ideas to the ones that we have already.

We can allow our undisciplined minds to determine the course of our lives, or we can learn to master our minds and enjoy a life of unbounded freedom. In order to live such a life, we need to start by emptying the teacup instead of adding more tea to it.

We need to learn how to empty our minds and start fresh. This is the purpose of Zen.

Zen is about polishing the mirror of our inner lives so that we can see it clearly. Unfortunately, most of us have unpolished mirrors, so we cannot see clearly. Because we cannot see clearly, we allow our minds to dictate how we live our lives. Our minds become the master, and we are its servant. You can learn to turn the tables and make your mind your servant; this is the purpose of Zen meditation.

This book is intended to be just an introduction to Zen. It represents the testing of the waters with your toes before entering a swimming pool. In truth, Zen cannot be understood by reading about it or listening to a lecture as Zen is beyond concepts. The purpose of Zen is to transcend concepts.

The minds of most people are too far removed from that which is the core of Zen. It is this reason why this book was written. It is meant to be a bridge between the intellectual and conceptual understanding that has governed our lives since the time we were children and a state of being that is characterized by unbounded freedom and wisdom.

Anyone can learn Zen; it is not some elite or esoteric teaching; rather, it is about having a direct experience with the truth of who you are and the world around you. All that it takes is the desire, patience, persistence, and an empty teacup.

A Brief History of Zen

Zen meditation was founded over 2,500 years ago in India by the historical Buddha, Siddhattha Gotama. The son of a king, Siddhattha Gotama, left the palace walls and ventured out on his own. He came to know suffering for the first time as he witnessed the sickness, aging, and death that surrounded him.

No longer sheltered from these daily realities, Siddhatta made it his life's mission to learn how to end suffering. He became the student of many teachers and excelled in the practices that they taught, yet he still was not able to find the answer he was looking for.

One day, Siddhattha, disregarded all the teachings he learned and decided to sit under the Bodi tree. He made the determination that he would not move from his position until he became enlightened. At some point, from the stillness and silence within him, Siddhattha became enlightened. Siddhattha became known as the "Buddha," which means to "awake," or to become enlightened.

After the Buddha's death, his teachings spread to China, where it was known as Cha'an. From China, his teachings continued to spread to Japan, where it was known as Zazen, which translates to "sitting meditation." Eventually, the Buddha's teachings became to be known as "Zen."

Zen is unlike any other form of Buddhism, or any other form of spirituality, in that it involves a complete transformation of how we process our experience of reality. Zen is about transcending all concepts and developing a direct experience with reality by focusing on the present. In Zen, there are no scriptures, no dogmas, or principles. Zen does not involve adopting a new belief system nor does it require faith. For this reason, Zen can be incorporated by anyone, regardless of their religious or spiritual beliefs.

The benefits of practicing Zen include all of those found in other forms of meditations while offering a deeper understanding of our own nature and that of existence itself. Like other forms of meditation, practicing Zen mediation can improve concentration, release stress, enhance the immune system, improve sleep, and reduce blood pressure.

The main reason why people practice Zen is because it offers the practitioner greater clarity in perceiving the nature of reality. Zen offers a view of life and ourselves that is free from the distortions created by the mind. When we can experience ourselves and the world free of such distortions, what remains is unbounded freedom and love.

Most of us are unaware of how our mental activity affects our experience of life and the resulting suffering that it causes. Before we discuss how the mind determines our experience of life, try this simple exercise:

1. *Find a quiet and comfortable place to sit.*
2. *Allow yourself to relax and close your eyes.*
3. *Spend sometime focusing on the inhalation and exhalation of your breath. Allow yourself to relax.*
4. *Now imagine a beautiful sunset, experience in as much detail as possible. If you have trouble visualizing, do not worry. Simply allow yourself to imagine a sunset in a way that works for you.*
5. *Now imagine a large tree. Just as with the sunset, try to make it as real as possible for you.*
6. *Now imagine a black cat. Try to make the image of the black cat as real as possible.*

7. *Now imagine an ice-cube. Make the image real for yourself.*
8. *Now open your eyes.*

During this brief exercise, you imagined a sunset, a tree, a black cat, and an ice-cube. Depending on your ability to visualize, your images may have been undefined or vivid. Regardless of how you experienced your visualizations, you did not confuse yourself for the images that you created. In other words, at no time did you mistake yourself for the sunset, the large tree, the black cat, or the ice cube. Your sense of self remained separate from the images you created.

While this ability to distinguish between yourself and the images that you created was obvious during this exercise, most of the time this is not the case. Almost every moment of our daily lives, we allow our mental activity to define how we experience ourselves and the world around us. The following are just a few examples of how our minds determine our experience of life:

- *You are caught in a traffic jam and running late for an important appointment versus relaxing on a Caribbean cruise.*
- *You are facing financial hardship and are at risk of losing your home versus learning that you have inherited $10 million dollars.*
- *You experience the death of a loved one versus holding your newborn child.*
- *You are contemplating suicide due to a sense of hopelessness versus feeling that you are embraced by love.*

Unlike visualizing a sunset, being late for an important appointment, fearing the loss your home or loved one, or contemplating suicide, has a vastly greater impact on us. While we most likely would not identify with our visualizations of a black cat, our sense of self could be deeply impacted by financial hardship, death, the birth of a child, the loss of hope, or feeling loved by the universe. The reason that the visualization exercise you just did does not impact your sense of self the way any of three examples could is due to the meaning that we give to our thoughts.

At the deeper levels of awareness, one finds that even the most extreme experience has no more potency over our lives than does the thought of a black cat or a large tree. It is the ability to rise above conceptual thought and experience the pure nakedness of reality that we discover that we and the universe are inseparable, that our individual lives are like eternal currents flowing through the ocean of existence. It is from this position of awareness that that we realize that all of experience, including our sense of personhood, is nothing more than an illusion.

Our thoughts are like mental lenses. When you look through a lens, you can only see that which is found within the field of the lens. If you look through a microscope, you are able to see only that which is within the field that the lens encompasses; you cannot see anything that lies beyond it. If I am looking through a pair of binoculars, I can see everything with the field of visibility that is allowed by the lenses. However, I cannot see what lies beyond the periphery of the lenses. Now consider the lens of tinted sunglasses. Whatever you look at will be the same color as the color of the tint used in the lenses. In the same manner, our thoughts restrict the scope of our awareness so that we only become aware of a fragment of the total experience that is available to us.

A belief is a thought that we are certain about. Because we are certain of our beliefs, the scope of our awareness becomes restricted to the scope of our beliefs. If I believe that people cannot be trusted, my awareness will be focused on all the reasons why people cannot be trusted. If I believe that somehow I am inadequate, my awareness will be focused on all the reasons why I am inadequate. Conversely, if I believe that I am successful person, my awareness will focus on all the reasons why I am successful. Whether our thoughts are positive or negative, they restrict our awareness to the infinite potential for experience that exist outside the realm of our thoughts.

Like tinted lenses, our thoughts create the meaning of our experiences. There is no inherent meaning to experience; rather, our thoughts create the meaning of our experiences. Our thoughts constrict our awareness of experience and impose meaning onto it. For this reason, our sense of self and our world is a product of the culmination of all our thoughts. Zen is about having a direct experience of experience, unfiltered by the functions of our mind. When you have this direct experience, you will start the process of mastering your mind instead of what you have done all your life, being a servant to your mind.

The World of Illusions

Think for a moment, what is the difference between a dream and waking reality? You may think that a dream is just imagined, while waking reality is the real thing. After all, in a dream we may be flying or be chased by a lion. While in our waking state, these things are improbable or impossible. Now consider deep sleep, that stage of sleep that we all crave for. When we are in deep sleep, we have no sense of experience of any aspect of existence, and we have no memory of it when we awaken. Every day, most of us travel back and forth between these three realms; yet, we treat only one of these realms, the waking state, as being real. We live out our lives believing that which we experience when we are awake is real, our dreams our imaginary, while the experience of deep sleep is offered little if any reflection by us. We just know that we want it.

If you talked to a Zen master, he or she would tell you that we have it all in reverse. Our waking state is just a dream; during deep sleep we experience the truth of existence, and that we are making the transition between the waking state to deep sleep when dreaming. In other words, our "waking state" is the dream, our dream state is when we begin to "wake up" and that we are fully awake in deep sleep.

In my stating that the waking state is really the dream state, and that deep sleep is the waking state, do not try to understand this using your intellect. The mind is incapable of grasping the non-phenomenal. To say something is phenomenal means that it can be perceived by the senses. Anyone who meditates understands that all mental activity is phenomenal. Thoughts, sensations, and perceptions are considered phenomenal. In fact, anything that can be experienced must be phenomenal.

Since the mind can only detect the phenomenal, anything that cannot be experienced is considered non-phenomenal. The importance of this understanding is that we never experience an objective world or reality; all of our experiences in life are but projections of the mind. In order to better understand this, let us imagine that we are looking at a rosebush in a garden. When we see the rosebush, we are not really seeing an entity called "rosebush" that exists outside ourselves. That which we perceive as being a rosebush is actually a mental construct or experience that is created by our brains.

Our five senses gather information from the environment and convert that information into electrical impulses. These impulses are then processed by the brain, which then constructs an experience that we call "rosebush." All of our experiences in life are created by the mind and experienced through the mind. Whether it is something that we are experiencing visually, through hearing, smelling, or through touch, all experiences are a product of electrical impulses within us. It is on the mental construct that we call "experience" that we impose a sense of meaning.

Meaning is created through the association of our mental experiences with the emotions or feelings that are occurring when we are having the experience. Going back to the example of the rosebush, a person creates a mental representation of a "rosebush" while at the same time experiencing a sensation that is the result of an emotion or feeling. Through the process of conditioning, the "rosebush" becomes associated with that sensation. In the future, when the person experiences a "rosebush," they will automatically experience the meaning. As a child, a person may be told by his or her parents "Look at that rosebush, isn't it beautiful." Later in life, this person may fall in love. Since roses are equated in our culture with romance, the positive feelings associated with roses are reinforced. When that person witnesses the happiness of their beloved, upon receiving the rose, then the meaning associated to roses becomes that much stronger. In terms of meaning, the only difference between this person and someone who is indifferent to roses lies in the emotions or feelings that they experienced when encountering the "rosebush."

To talk about Zen is to talk about consciousness, and as previously stated, the rational mind cannot grasp the non-phenomenal. The use of language to discuss consciousness or Zen is at best limiting and at worst a barrier. Because of this, everything that I have just written is inaccurate. At deeper levels of awareness, one realizes that there is no Zen, no mind, no rose, and no sensations. There is no e-book, and there is no one reading this e-book. In fact, there is no "you."

Anything we can perceive, experience, or identify with is just another concept of the mind. This is why a Zen master would tell you that deep sleep is the wakened state and that what we call being "awake" is a dream. Everything that we experience when we are "awake" is a product of our minds. Because we do not experience the mind (or anything else for that matter) during deep sleep, it offers us the purest "experience" of ultimate reality.

You maybe thinking "What good is it if my purest experience of reality occurs in deep sleep when I am unable to experience it?" This type of thinking is also a product of the mind. In fact, being "awake," "deep sleep," "reality," and "experience" are also concepts; they only exist in our mind. Know that you can experience "pure consciousness" and freedom from the mind; many have accomplished this. All that you need to do is have the desire, the persistence, and the patients. It is also important to note that you do not have to go to a monastery; you do not have to find a guru, and you do not have to change the way you live. You can remain a productive person and take care of your responsibilities; you can still engage and experience daily life, and you do not have to give-up anything except your fears, anxiety, and sense of limitation. You also need to be willing to accept ultimate freedom, unbounded love, and a profound sense of peace. Any takers?

Lifting the Veil of Illusions

Zen is about experiencing all the phenomena that we call "experience" and realizing that they are just illusionary, including your sense of being a person. But before we go much deeper in this idea, it is about time that we do a few exercises in order to develop greater understanding.

1. *Sit down and take a look around you. Where ever you may be, notice everything that is around you.*
2. *Now close your eyes and allow yourself to relax.*
3. *I want you to place your awareness on your breath. While breathing normally, place your focus on the sensations of your breath. Be aware of the air entering your body during inhalation and when it leaves your body during exhalation. Allow yourself to relax.*
4. *I want you to imagine that you are an alien from another galaxy. You have been sent to Earth to gather information about this planet. You have absolutely no information about Earth; it is completely unknown to you. You have no sense of concepts, names or words that would allow you to*

describe your experience here. The only thing that you can do is to observe with out forming any conclusions, analysis, or comparisons. The only thing that you can do is to be an observer of experience.

5. *Now open yours eyes and look around again. Is your experience of your surroundings different from your first look?*

If you do not see any difference from your first observations of your surroundings, repeat this exercise until you notice a difference.

For this next exercise, it is important to not rely on your knowledge, your education, or your past experience, be a blank slate and rely only on your direct experience.

1. *Look at any object that is in your surroundings.*
2. *As you look at the object, determine if the act of seeing stops at a certain point and the object being viewed begins,*

or does the object and the act of seeing flow into each other?

3. *Now determine if seeing occur from within you or from outside of you.*
4. *Now determine if there is awareness of the object being viewed.*
5. *Does the object occur within awareness or is awareness within the object?*
6. *Now determine if there is awareness of the act of seeing.*
7. *Does the act of seeing occur within awareness or is awareness found within seeing?*
8. *Now determine if there is any separation between awareness, seeing, and the object, or are they all one in the same?*

Here is the last exercise for this chapter. As in the previous exercise, approach it as a blank slate, relying only on your direct experience.

1. *Sit down and close your eyes. Focus on your breathe as you did in the previous exercise.*
2. *Keeping your eyes closed, I want you to touch the chair that you are sitting on.*
3. *Relying on your direct experience, determine if you are touching the chair, or are experiencing the sensation of the chair?*

My hope is that through these exercises that you arrived at the understanding that any form of separation between you and your experience is just illusionary. I also hope you come to the conclusion that all of experience is an extension of awareness.

When you look at an object, that object is not independent of you; rather, it is an aspect of your awareness, just as is the act of seeing. In other words, you, the act of seeing, and the object being seen are one in the same, there is no distinction other than that which occurs in the mind.

When you touched the chair, you did not touch the chair; the chair is just a concept in your mind. What you experienced was a sensation, a sensation that we have been taught to call "chair." If you have any problems coming to these conclusions, do not get frustrated. Simply practice these exercises without "trying" or "striving" to accomplish anything; just pay attention to your experience.

Zen: The Importance of Clear Seeing

Before we go any further, let us discuss the significance of practicing Zen. All the problems of humankind are a product of our minds.

Because we see ourselves as separate entities from the rest of life, we experience it as a threat or as a resource to be used. We engage in wars; we kill each other; we exploit each other; we dominate those we feel are inferior to us; we pollute the environment, and destroy the natural world. Because we identify with our thoughts, emotions, and perceptions, we become them. We become our hate; we become our insecurity; we become our fear; we become our anxiety; we become our sense of hopelessness, and we become our doubt.

 It is also true that we become our love, our joy, and our compassion; however, none of this is dependable. For most of us, our sense of self is like a roller coaster ride, as our thoughts and emotions fluctuate based on what is happening in our environment.

If we get a raise or find a new love, we are happy. If we lose our job or our relationship falls apart, we become fearful, angry, or feel insecure. As long as we allow our sense of well-being to be dependent on what is happening in our world, we will never know true freedom.

True freedom, unbounded love and compassion, and profound inner peace become our experience when we come to the realization of our true nature, which is non-phenomenal. This is why Zen masters speak of deep sleep as being the state of being truly awake. While in deep sleep, there is no self-identification with anything that is phenomenal.

When we are in deep sleep, we are not thinking of how we goofed up the previous day; we are not feeling anxious or concerned about what may happen in the future, and we are not thinking about the list of things that we have to do. In fact, we are free of thought. Not only are we free of thought, we are free of ourselves; we lose our connection with the physical body and the mind. In deep sleep, we enjoy unbounded freedom where there is nothing to do, nothing is missing, and nothing needs to be gained.

When we can incorporate this state of being in our daily lives, life takes on a whole new quality. We become a witness to all of life with retaining a deep sense of peace and equanimity. We realize that we are an aspect of all of experience and that all of experience is one.

The truth of our being is that of awareness. We are the one that is the knower of all experience. Hopefully you experienced this in the earlier exercise where you were asked to look at an object and determine if the act of seeing is separate from the object being seen.

In reference to the past exercises, I hope you also experienced a sense that there is no distinct separation between you, the act of seeing, and the object being seen. All of these are an aspect of experience. They are in separable, flowing into each other.

If enough people understood Zen, then the need for government, for laws, for a military, or the police would not be needed. Each one of us would behave in a way that honors all of life, including ours.

Who Are You?

We will start off this chapter with a meditation whose purpose is to bring you to a greater level awareness as to the nature of who you are. Do the following:

1. *Find a comfortable place to sit, and close your eyes. Try to keep your back as straight as possible while remaining relaxed and comfortable.*
2. *As in the previous exercises, focus on the sensations of your breath, making sure that you are breathing normally.*
3. *It is important that while you are doing this meditation that you put absolutely no effort into what you doing. For most us, we are so conditioned to try to achieve a certain result, or we have expectations of what we should be experiencing. When this happens, we either start doubting ourselves or become frustrated. I want you to completely accept whatever arises in your experience, don't try to*

change anything. There is no such thing as getting it right or wrong.

4. *As you observe your breathe, you will experience thoughts, sensations, feelings, and sounds. Let them come and go on their own accord.*

5. *Anytime your mind wanders, gently return it to your breathing.*

6. *As you continue to focus on your breath, you will notice your mind will become more still, more quiet. It is important to note that before reaching this calm, you will most likely experience a burst of activity in your mind. Do not get distracted by this as it is natural. If and when this happens, just continue to focus on your breath until your mind calms down.*

7. *As your continue observing your breath, you will notice that it will take less of our attention to observe it; you will not have to remind yourself to focus on it. This is an indication that you have gone to a deeper level of awareness.*

8. *Relax your attention and simply observe whatever comes into your awareness. Notice how thought, sensation, emotions, and feelings arise from the depths of your awareness and then fade away. Nothing that you can experience is permanent; all phenomena are transient and in constant flux. Thoughts appear and the fade away. Sensations and emotions change in their level of intensity. Even if you here a sound that is continuous, it will fluctuate in its intensity.*

9. *Allow yourself to experience everything that comes into the light of your awareness; offer complete acceptance to all of your experiences. Do not at any point of this mediation use*

your imagination or create a meaning for your experience. Let all of your experiences come and go on their own accord.

10. *Notice that you are aware of thought but that you are not thought. You are aware of sensation but that you are not sensation. You experience feelings but you are not feelings. When you have a troubling thought, awareness is not troubled. You may be feeling peaceful, but awareness is neither peaceful nor disturbed. You are aware of all experience yet awareness is untouched by all of experience.*

11. *Who is the one that is aware of experience? Can you reveal the identity of the one that is aware? Search for the one that is aware. Who is this one? You may say "I am the one that is aware," or "consciousness is aware," or "my higher power is aware." To say any of these things requires awareness of them as well. How can these be the source of awareness when awareness is required to know of their*

existence? In fact, regardless of how you answer this question, there must be awareness of it. Thoughts of "I", "me," "spirit," "soul," or "higher power," are simply that, thoughts. Keep searching, do not give up. Try to find the one that is the source of awareness.

The Center of the Universe is called "I"

Long before you could speak or walk, you had a sense of "I." The sense of "I" is the most fundamental aspect of our existence. You never have to remind yourself that you exist; the knowing that you exist is instantaneous. You may forget your car keys; you may forget your spouse's birthday, but you will never forget that you exist. This sense of existence is what we call "I."

When we do not have a contemplative practice, such as meditation, the sense of "I" personalizes and identifies with our sense of experience. When this happens, you claim the thoughts that you experience as "your thoughts." You claim all sensations as "your sensations." You claim your body, your mind, your relationships, your possessions, and your perspective. If you are depressed, you claim "I" am depressed. If you are experiencing despair, you claim "I" am in despair. If you a feeling superior, you claim "I" am right.

When we personalize "I," we take on the weight of the universe as our sense of self is constantly being impacted by the phenomena that we call experience. Every thought, every action, every sensation, every perception, every belief, every encounter, and every relationship becomes attached to our sense of self. Practicing Zen allows us to observe the sense of "I" so that we can gain some objectivity toward it, rather than getting sucked up by it.

If you felt confident with the previous exercises, the next exercise will challenge you to go even further into awareness. If you did not feel comfortable with the previous exercises, please practice them, until you feel comfortable with them, before attempting the next exercise.

Start off as you did in the previous exercises by focusing on your breathing. Allow yourself to observe the coming and going of phenomena; observe the thoughts, perceptions, and sensations that appear in your awareness. When you mind is calm, and you can comfortably observe the phenomena of your mind, try to locate the one that you refer to as "I."

Can you find the one that you refer to as "I"? Where is this "I" that has dominated your life since you were a small child, that has dominated humanity? What does this "I" look like? What form does it take? Does it appear as an image, a sensation, stillness, or emptiness?

If you believe that you have found "I," then keep looking. Do not get analytical about it. Do not imagine anything. Go only by your direct experience. If you are unable to find "I," do not worry. This is good news. If you believe you have found that which you refer to "I," then I have a question for you. That which you take to be "I," what is aware of it?

The truth of the matter is that what ever you refer to as being "I," is simply another phenomena. Who you are is not "I." That which you refer to as "I" is just a thought. The only difference between the "I" thought and any other thought that you have is that you believe it to be you. You have a profound identification with it.

That which is aware of "I" is also aware of all phenomena. After all, something can only exist if there is awareness to perceive it. The truth of who you are is so great that the existence of all phenomena is dependent on your awareness of it.

Zen practice allows to us gain greater clarity to our true nature. The Bhagavad-Gita refers to the nature of the true self in the following passage:

"Weapons do not cut it; fire does not burn it,

Waters do not wet it, wind does not wither it.

It cannot be cut or burned; it cannot be wet or withered;

It is enduring, all-pervasive, fixed, immovable, and timeless."

Your true nature cannot be understood through concepts or through the use of intellectual thinking. Your true nature cannot be communicated through the use of language. This is why the proceeding passage from the Bhagavad-Gita does not attempt to describe the true self, which is impossible. Instead, it relies on the use of words, which are concepts, to point to that which the true self is not. Anything that you can perceive, think, feel, hear, or smell is not your true self; your true self-cannot be experienced.

Who you are is the one that cannot be experienced, yet is aware of all phenomena. That which you identify as being you, the person, is just another phenomenon perceived by the true self. With practice and patients, practicing Zen will bring you to this discovery. When this happens, your whole sense of relationship with both yourself and the world around you will take a dramatic shift. An analogy for this transformation is the sky. The sky is vast; it is endless. Beneath the sky are clouds that take on a wide range of shape and sizes. The sky is unaffected by clouds which are in constant motion as they transverse the vast sky. Your true nature is the sky while the clouds are your perceptions, thoughts, feelings, emotions and other phenomena. As with the sky, you can enjoy the vastness and stillness of your being as the clouds of your mind's projections transverse the sky of your pure awareness.

We establish ourselves in the position of the true self when we allow ourselves to soak in the waters of stillness and silence that comes from practicing Zen. Zen allows us to develop the clarity of awareness that leads to the realization that we are the witness of all phenomena, of all experience. The clouds of our mental projections can no longer disturb us as we have the direct knowing that who we are is the eternal sky that is witnessing the coming and going of our minds "clouds."

The "I" is not a mistake nor is it a liability. If we did not have a sense of "I," we would be without experience, just as in deep sleep. The sense of "I" allows us to have experience. Problems only occur when we identify ourselves with "I."

A metaphor for our relationship with "I" is going to movies. When you go to the movies, you experience scenes that are dramatic, scary, or emotional. If these very same scenes actually occurred to us in real life, we would most likely become deeply consumed by them. When you watch a movie, you may still have an emotional reaction; however, you realize it is just a movie so you do not take it seriously. Watching the movie is a metaphor for practicing Zen. Without elevating our awareness, we confuse the movie as being the reality of our lives. We experience the movie as real life because of the personalizing of "I."

All experiences serve a purpose in the expansion of consciousness. There is nothing in this universe that it is an "accident" or a "mistake." Everything that exists plays a role in the expansion of our own happiness.

In order to better understand how everything plays a role in the expansion of our happiness, let's return to the notion of deep sleep, that part of our lives that is void of experience. Pure consciousness, sometimes called universal consciousness, is characterized by "oneness." Just as in deep sleep, there is no distinction or sense of separation in pure consciousness.

The only way purse consciousness can experience itself is for it to differentiate itself by manifesting itself as phenomena. This can be better understood if we think of the water cycle. Imagine air as pure consciousness. Just as pure consciousness, the air is undefined in that one portion of air is identical to any other portion. When the right circumstances occur, the moisture in the air condenses and results in rain. If the rain cools enough, it becomes ice. Both the rain and ice are distinct and separate expressions of the formless moisture in the air. Pure consciousness is to the air as water and ice are to all phenomena, including our minds and bodies. It is through this sense of separation that gives rise to experience. In this manner, you are multidimensional being as you are pure consciousness who is at the same time a physical being, a physical being who is able to have experience with other phenomena.

It is thorough your experience that pure consciousness learns about itself; consciousness is learning of itself through you. It is through such learning that leads to the expansion of both pure consciousness (i.e., the universe) and you. By committing yourself to Zen practice, all of that which has been written in this book will become self-evident. With this understanding, you will experience a profound shift in how you perceive yourself and the world around you. You will come to understand what it is to live without fear or a sense of limitation. You will be able to access profound wisdom, and enjoy a sense of connection to all of existence. You will know intimately what was meant by the bible passage: "In this world but not of it."

Zen in Daily Life

Practicing Zen allows to us untangle ourselves from the sense of "I"; we do not get caught up with concepts or thoughts. We can transcend the intellectual mind and experience life with greater clarity. Zen allows us to free ourselves from the distortions that thoughts, perceptions, and sensations have on our experience of reality.

It is important to note that there is nothing inherently wrong with any aspect of our experience. Mental phenomena such as thoughts, memories, emotions, feelings, and the mind are all expressions of consciousness. Even the ego, which many spiritual teachings dismiss as being a burden to the achievement of happiness, is an aspect of consciousness.

Zen does not mean hiding from the world or disowning it. Nor does it mean you give up your life as you know it (unless you desire to do so). On the contrary, your experience of life becomes more intimate, more joyful--more magical. Just as it is impossible to describe the experience of Zen in writing, so is it impossible to describe all the changes and benefits that you can experience from Zen. Zen will affect every aspect of your being as you will be perceiving life differently. Because you are no longer tangled up with sense of "I", your sense of "I" will diminish. Next time you think to yourself "I need to do this" or "I am worried" or "I made a mistake," you may start smiling as you realize that this "I" is not you; it is just a thought in your head.

The diminishing sense of identification with "I" will make you feel more peaceful as all concerns, frustrations, and worries are dependent on you identifying with "I."

You may, at this point, have concerns that losing your sense of "I" will result in you becoming detached from life, in becoming less responsible, or feeling less motivated. In fact, the opposite is true. Because you will be less identified with the sense of "I", you will begin the free yourself from ego-ic thinking. In doing so, you will experience things more deeply while at the same time not personalizing it. You will experience greater appreciation, greater sensitivity, and greater compassion for all beings.

While your sense of connection with others will strengthen, you will not feel a sense of dependency upon them. You experience total freedom in being yourself, while allowing others to do the same. Expectations of others will fade away as you will no longer feel dependent on others meeting your expectations. You will not have expectations of others because you will realize the absolute completeness of your own being. Your relationships become based solely on the sense of connection that you have with others.

Other benefits of Zen are that your sense of past and future will fade away as your awareness becomes increasingly centered on the present moment. The amount of time that you spend anticipating what may happen in the future, or your reflecting back on what happened in the past, will become less as become increasingly aware of what is happening in the present moment.

This does not mean that you do not plan for the future or take time to learn from the past; rather, you will do these things intentionally, and when you do, you will not get caught up there.

One of the biggest benefits of Zen is that you take life less seriously. When you realize that which you call "I" is just and a thought, and that who you are is the awareness of thought, there comes a sense of peace and stillness. Instead of seeing yourself as a person who has life happening to them, you have the understanding that you are the witness of all of life. You are the silent witness who is aware of the mind, the body, the sense of "I", of perceptions, of sensations, of sound, of taste, and of all phenomena. Who you are is even aware of awareness. Who you are is eternal, non-local, and non-physical. What is there to worry about?

You will have the knowing that what others call "daily" life is just an illusion, of which you willingly take part in. Because of this understanding, you will experience greater love, compassion, and connection with others as all sense of fear, even of death, begin to dissolve.

Because Zen allows us to free ourselves from conceptual thinking, we can contribute to our world with a level of creativity and wisdom that is most rare. Practicing Zen puts what we call "problems" in a whole new light, as does the way we address them. In order to better understand this, let us say that you are having a conflict with another person. Without practicing Zen, most people would attribute the problem to how the other person is behaving. At the level of everyday awareness, you see this person as a separate person whose actions or way of thinking is causing you frustration.

Your sense of happiness in this relationship is dependent on this other person thinking or behaving in a manner that is consistent with your expectations. In order to influence this person, you may express your disapproval, ignore them, or become vindictive toward them.

By recognizing that "I" is just a thought, you will stop taking yourself so seriously. At the same time you realize that this other person identifies with "I." With this awareness, you will naturally feel greater compassion for them. You can become aware of all the concepts held by you and this other person, identify which ones are causing you and the other person to suffer, and approach the situation with wisdom. You will not have to think of how to solve the problem; the answer to the problem will become self-evident. Just this realization will allow you to respond to the other person in away that is natural spontaneous, and non-threatening to them. You will be able to touch their heart without any expectations from them.

Bonus Chapter
The Joy of Mindfulness

"Feelings come and go like clouds in a windy sky. Conscious breathing is my anchor."
— Thich Nhat Hanh

What is Mindfulness Anyway?

Mindfulness is a behavior we can learn to help us in some odd moments of a challenging day. It is also potentially a central part of a way of life that can transform you from a somewhat unhappy, struggling person to someone who is usually happy and optimistic and can handle the pains, pangs, and joy of living well. Truly!

There is some general confusion about mindfulness and meditation which it is helpful to clear up first. Meditation is a practice where you set some time aside to focus quietly. The purpose is to do something positive for yourself by connecting with yourself again and centering so that you can become calm with a clear mind. Mindfulness is expressly about focusing on the present moment. It is one style of meditation, and that is where the confusion has arisen.

Many people use the words interchangeably, and maybe that doesn't matter as the point of all the other types of meditation and of mindfulness itself, is to bring us to a place of happiness and reality. A place where we are accepting of Life as it is.

The Important connection with Emotions

"Feelings come and go like clouds...." Says Thich Naht Hanh

The rise in interest and use of mediation has been meteoric in the last twenty years. As the number of stressors in our lives has grown with the multiple forms of communication available and financial demands, have increased with recessions and money market volatility, more doctors are prescribing 'meditation' as a stress management tool. It is a healthier option than Valium! It helps us manage that swirling soup of emotion and unhelpful behaviors and habits we have developed to help us cope.

However it isn't an easier option for it requires commitment and practice, and that is where many people give up. Ironically in a life that has so many demands, when they most need to slow down and center, they say they have no time to do the practice! However for those who do take their quality of life and their health seriously, it is a commitment that has quite amazing results.

One of the very common difficulties people have with stress management is actually not with the stressors themselves. It is with their emotional management as their levels of anxiety, fear, frustration or overwhelm take over and they can't find beneficial ways to control these feelings. They then begin to sublimate them; distract themselves, eat more, develop addictive behaviors, turn to comfort food, nicotine, alcohol… as an attempt to distance themselves from their very uncomfortable feelings.

When we are in the grip of an emotional state, it seems to take us over, and we start to think that the feeling is what we are. "I'm so frustrated I could scream." "I'm anxious all the time." It becomes very difficult to recognize that these are temporary emotions which are blocking our capacity to think and listen. And that, in fact., we have a very creative mind which could problem solve the situation pretty well if we could get it to be clear enough to start working.

And this is where meditation comes in. Through taking up one of the forms of mediation such as TM (Transcendental Meditation), Insight Mediation, Walking Mediation, Zen Meditation…. or

Mindfulness Mediation we can start to quieten down. This means we can still our crazy 'monkey mind,' listen to the intuitive voice inside and separate ourselves out from the emotional turmoil caused by too many stress hormones. We can begin to think again....

Other benefits of Mindfulness and meditation

Spiritual Awakening

There are other reasons to meditate, not only to help with stress management. For thousands of years, people have used meditation as a pathway to Awakening themselves spiritually. Buddhists have been using MindfulMediation for centuries and Thich Nhat Hahn, a modern Buddhist monk, has brought the practice to the Western world in a very accessible way. For those of you who have an interest in this pathway and strive to live in a way that keeps you connected with the Divine, Mindfulness practice is a very lovely method of being open to life, glorying in the beauty of it and living every moment fully and authentically.

Emotional Healing

Sadly many people have experienced some kind of trauma in their lives or have struggled with the pain of emotions that they cannot get away from such as shame, guilt, severe anxiety. Sometimes these emotional states have lead to mental health issues such as depression. For people in that kind of state, the practice of mindfulness meditation can be a lifeline. It sets up conditions in the mind, body, and soul that allow the person to enter the trauma or the pain equipped to manage it differently and better.

Used in this way Mindfulness is a very powerful healer and is particularly effective used in conjunction with psychotherapy or counseling so that the person can make sense of what is happening.

Best Mindfulness Tip

Let's turn to one of the most influential and respected Zen Buddhist monks of our time, Thich Nhat Hanh, and take inspiration from what he says about mindful living. This is taken from his books on "The Art of Mindful Living".

"Mindfulness is the capacity to be aware of what is going on and what is there. The object of your mindfulness can be anything." We are always aware – in fact, we are awareness itself.

Thich Nhat Hanh carries on, "You can look at the sky, breathe in, and say:

"Breathing in, I am aware of the blue sky." Then you can add "With each breath I come back to the present moment."

Conclusion

In concluding this book, we will close with one more Zen tale. A boy was searching the mountains in hopes to find a Zen master who lived there. When the boy found the Zen master, he explained to him that he wanted to understand Zen. The Zen master took the boy to a neighboring spring and had him sit on a rock. The Zen master then asked the boy "What do you hear?" The boy replied, I hear the rushing waters of the stream." The Zen master then told the boy to put all of his attention on the sound of the stream. After a while, the boy became perplexed. He then asked the Zen master, "Master, what if my answer to your question was not the stream? What would have had happened if I told you that what I heard was the birds singing instead?" The Zen master replied, "I would have told you to put all of your attention on the sound of the singing birds."

Later on toward the evening, the Zen master took the body out into an open field. Together they watched a beautiful full moon. The Zen master called his dog, which came running toward them. The Zen master pointed his finger to the moon and told his dog "Look at the moon." The dog just fixated on his owner's pointing finger.

These two stories point out to simplicity of Zen practice; it is us that make it seem difficult to practice. Just as with the story of the river, we spend our lives looking all over for our sense of peace or happiness, never understanding that all the answers to our questions are available to us where we find ourselves at this moment. We do not need to chase our answers by changing careers, relationships, or where we live. Our answers can be found wherever our attention is being directed. We do not have to change our world; we just need to look more deeply where we find ourselves now.

Just as the dog looked at the Zen master's finger instead of the full moon, we are preoccupied with the pointers to wisdom instead of wisdom itself. So many people pursue different religions, spiritual practices, or philosophies in hope of finding inner peace. What we do not understand is that all of these things are just like the Zen master's finger. Instead of looking at the beauty of the full moon, we are preoccupied with the belief system. There is nothing wrong with learning about different belief systems as they do provide value, though only temporarily.

Beliefs are just like the pointing finger; they lack any inherent power. Anything that we learn is just pointing us to something even more profound, something that is beyond our ability to comprehend.

Our lives can be so much simpler and more joyful if we stop looking for our answers and learn to look more deeply within. Life is like a grand masquerade party that is being attended by billions of guests, each wearing their own unique looking costume and mask. Some dress like our mates, spouses, family members, or friends. Some dress like strangers, while others dress like animals, plants, mountains, oceans, or rocks.

Whatever you can experience in life, there is someone dressed-up like it. In the final hour of the party, everyone is told to take off their masks and reveal their true identity. It is then that we find the same face is behind every mask that is removed. That face is the face of the Self, of consciousness.

My hope for this world is that we all rejoice at this party and enjoy the diversity and creativity that abounds everywhere. My hope is that we will learn to treasure the richness of experience that we call "life." Finally, my hope is that you will never forget the one behind the mask, for this One is the only truth, and this One is you...

If you enjoyed this book and found something to experiment with, try out, share or commit to we are delighted.

Health and happiness can be found through many avenues and for all of them the journey itself is usually the joy. The destination is what we want to achieve, but it is in getting there that we constantly find out more about ourselves and our own uniqueness. And this is the most fascinating of all.

Until we meet again in another book – be healthy, be happy, be beautiful inside and out.

Sending you lots of love from here,

Maya Faro

For similar books, visit:

www.YourWellnessBooks.com

and

www.LOAforSuccess.com

www.ingramcontent.com/pod-product-compliance
Lightning Source LLC
Chambersburg PA
CBHW042120100526
44587CB00025B/4136